HOW TO USE THE POWER OF YOUR POSITIVE THINKING

Introduction

Eventually in your life, you've likely found out about the force of positive reasoning. Fundamentally, this is a hypothesis that battles assuming you accept beneficial things will happen to you, there will be some kind of calamitous change in the energies encompassing you which will really make beneficial things happen to you. For as many individuals who have faith in the force of positive reasoning, there are a lot more who accept it's each of the a lot of New Age pop brain research claptrap or glossed over Peter Dish clichés.

Here is the kicker: they're okay.

Positive reasoning is an arrangement of convictions. So in the event that you accept it doesn't work-then, obviously, it won't work. Furthermore, in the event that you accept it does work...well, you understand. For non-devotees, utilizing positive reasoning is like attempting to find a new line of work after secondary school. You want insight to find a new line of work, yet you really want something important to get the experience. It tends to be hard to tell where you should begin. However, very much like some other interaction, the way to making positive reasoning work for you is to begin little. Sow seeds, maybe, and afterward figure out how to tend and develop those seeds until you have a psychological nursery that bears a wonderful harvest, a large number of years. The sky is the limit with positive thinking.

Norman Vincent Peale, the dad of positive reasoning, once said: "On the off chance that you have zing and excitement you draw in zing and energy. Life offers back in kind." This is the substance of positive reasoning. It's not such a lot of a hypothesis as it is an infectious illness. Similarly as outrage and antagonism spread rapidly from one individual to another, humour do as well and bliss just positive sentiments spread far quicker. Consider it: have you at any point saw that the fastest method for facilitating what is happening is to make a joke? The moment somebody giggles or grins, a good feeling spreads through everybody nearby. Regardless of whether the maddened gatherings feel improved, they are essentially ready to examine the issue in a disconnected and objective manner, and move on as opposed to harping on pessimism. For that equivalent explanation, solo drivers who get removed in rush hour gridlock will generally stay furious for essentially the remainder of the drive-since there is no other person close to them to convey great vibrations and break the pressure. Appears to be legit, right?

On the off chance that you've gotten this book and perused this far, the seeds of conviction are as of now there. Your subsequent stage is to get your psyche's nursery free from uncertainty and prepare to plant. You'll figure out how to take all that antagonism and mulch it down into compost that will allow your conceivable outcomes to develop.

Presently get your digging tool, and we should go to the nursery.

The greatest tree on the planet develops from a seed you can hold between two fingers.

"Whether you want to or whether you assume you can't...you're correct."

- Henry Passage

Sowing YOUR SEEDS

"In each peculiarity the starting remaining parts generally the most eminent second."

- Thomas Carlyle

To check out the force of positive reasoning, you ought to presumably begin little especially in the event that you don't really accept that it will work. It's one thing to tell yourself, "Tomorrow, when I get up in the first part of the day I won't hit nap multiple times and feel sleepy until the end of the day," and very one more to tell yourself, "Tomorrow, when I get up toward the beginning of the day I'll be living freely rich and living in a chateau." (Except if, obviously, you are as a matter of fact autonomously well off and living in a manor right now; in which case you could attempt to think your direction into responsibility for little country.)

The most common way of making positive reasoning work for you starts with obliteration, or if nothing else a gentle change in your thinking structure. To account for new techniques and thoughts, you should initially remove all the old cynicism designs you've been working all through your life. For some's purposes, this can be a progressive interaction: as you witness positive reasoning work for you, each little move toward turn, you will gradually get out those beneficial things-just happen-to-others considerations, and have the option to develop the seeds of progress.

Roots: What's In Your Nursery Now?

"The best transformation of our age is the revelation that people, by changing the internal perspectives of their psyches, can change the external parts of their lives."

- William James

What's keeping you down? Indeed, even the individuals who completely embrace the hypothesis of good reasoning might feel a few doubts over entrusting their lives to simple idea. There are numerous conceivable outcomes that could be delivering weeds in your psychological nursery, and the most ideal way to dispose of a weed is to yank it out, roots what not. In this part we'll examine probably the most widely recognized hindrances individuals experience making a course for positive reasoning, as well as how to beat them and establish the groundwork for a solid life standpoint.

Confidence: Contracting the I-Love-Me Sickness

For the greater part of human life, confidence was an inconceivable thought much the same as the speculations of those blasphemers who accepted the world was round. The expression "confidence" - characterized by Webster's Word reference as "pride in oneself; dignity" - disclosed its direction into the not unexpected mindfulness during the '60s and '70s as a catch-all term to depict the quintessence of nurturing issues. The "old ways" of nurturing were articulated savage and harming to the sprouting confidence of our childhood, and many guardians unfortunate of bringing up troubled, not well changed kids accepted exhortation that prompted an age of youngsters with high self-esteem...so high it obscured moral obligation and made a "me-first" mind-set.

Then again, the vast majority of us are instructed that respecting ourselves is a vain, self-cantered and bothersome quality. Counsel advising us to rest easier thinking about ourselves and sporadically put us initially appears to be illogical, best case scenario. All things considered, isn't self-esteem the initial step headed for Inner self Focal? Many individuals need to feel quite a bit better about themselves, however responsibility over and over again reappears and prevents solid confidence from creating.

In light of these clashing perspectives, confidence is a precarious little feeling to control. Finding some kind of harmony among humility and greed is significant. It takes practice to persuade yourself that you are a beneficial and meriting individual, while simultaneously remembering that you're not the focal point of the universe. However it might sound unimaginable, it's really easy to achieve.

Where do you rate on the confidence o-meter? The accompanying test will assist you with checking your sentiments and recognize regions that need improvement.

Me-ology: The Confidence Dipstick

To rate your confidence, pick the response that most intently mirrors your possible response to the accompanying circumstances:

1. You know you're great at making data sets. Your manager asks you and a few colleagues for a worker to sort out another client data information base, and one more worker to compose an organization bulletin which you have no clue about how to do.

A. Volunteer for both, on the grounds that you're so splendid you'll have the option to sort it out - even to the detriment of humiliating the organization the initial not many times you compose a horrendous pamphlet.

B. Volunteer for the data set and when Fred Jones additionally chips in, delicately call attention to that you've had more insight, however would be glad to show him what you know as you come.

C. Stay quiet. In any case, another person is without a doubt greater at it than you, and the manager could never pick you.

2. You're out with companions and you've quite recently passed gas uproariously in the centre of an eatery, so you:

A. Promptly fault a passing server or another person at your table. You are totally serious in your allegations, and it's absolutely impossible that anybody will actually want to nail it to you. Looking at the situation objectively, you'll allow them to have it.

B. Tell a wisecrack about that four-bean salad you had for lunch.

C. Endeavour to slither under the table, then excuse yourself and make a beeline for the washroom. You can't confront any of them until the end of the evening, and you consider paying the whole check at this moment and leaving before they notice you're gone-in the event that they notice you're no more.

3. At the point when you watch Peril or play Questions and answers, you:

A. Chuckle at different players when they find the solutions wrong. You know them all, and on the off chance that you at any point went on Risk you'd wipe them out.

B. Have a ton of fun. You know a portion of the responses and attempt to speculate about the rest. You love to learn new things.

C. Try not to watch Risk or play Questions and answers. You're not shrewd enough for stuff like that.

4. You've chosen to pursue that advancement at work. You:

A. Make a lot of others look terrible so it's basically impossible that you'll be missed.

B. Tell your supervisor you're keen on the advancement, and afterward set forth an additional energy to demonstrate you're great for the position.

C. Settle on the drive to work that you won't let it all out all things considered. You will not get it regardless of what you do, so it's an exercise in futility to attempt.

5. While pursuing a difficult choice, you:

A. Pick the choice that sounds best for you right now, and afterward adhere to your choice regardless of anything else, regardless of whether it ends up being some unacceptable one.

B. Gauge your choices and ponder the benefits and disservices of every one preceding settling on your last decision, however stay open to change in the event that it turns out there is a superior way.

C. Choices? You can't decide. You generally get some unacceptable thing and wind making everybody hopeless. You'll get another person to choose.

6. You're confronted with a whole night alone. You:

A. Boast, since you don't need to invest energy in that frame of mind of those hopeless idiots who believe they're your companions, yet can't compare to your splendid and shimmering character. In any case, you realize they're all lounging around wanting to hang with you.

B. Find opportunity to accomplish something you appreciate, similar to scrub down, read a decent book, or fix yourself your #1 supper.

C. Can't. You're too apprehensive about messing things up to think, so you will generally chip away at projects in short explodes and frequently wind up completing things late in light of the fact that you're so diverted.

8. A companion acquaints you with another person. You:

A. Demonstrate that you're a superior individual by offering something clever or shrewd that tells them your companion is focusing on you at the present time, not them. Assuming that the new individual is valuable, they'll put forth the attempt to get to know you.

B. Welcome that person heartily, present yourself and pose an unconditional inquiry, for example, "How would you make ends meet?" or "Where do you live?" You're ready to really stand by listening to the response and will save judgment until you get to realize the individual better.

C. Murmur "hi," and afterward sneak off looking for a companion who's not conversing with somebody you don't have any idea. Whoever the new individual is, they would have no desire to get to know you at any rate.

9. You stroll in to your home and you're welcomed by a horrendous odour: the cooler is turned off, and all that in it is ruined. You:

A. Quickly accept somebody was messing around with it and send off an examination to track down the guilty party.

B. First fitting it back in to see whether it actually works, and afterward attempt to sort out what occurred. In the event that another person was liable for turning off it, they can assist you with clearing it out. Regardless, you'll do what's important to address the issue.

C. Conclude you probably accomplished something wrong, and presently tormenting you is returning. You protest faintly as you clear out the fridge and can't help thinking about why things like this generally need to happen to you.

10. Your boss calls you into the workplace to praise you on the huge work you're doing on your new venture. You:

A. Say thanks to him obviously, meanwhile believing it's no time like the present he saw how incredible you are. Perhaps currently you'll get the regard you merit.

B. Are genuinely complimented, and tell him so. You additionally inquire as to whether there is whatever you might improve.

C. Demand that you're not actually doing all that admirably, and attempt to speed him up so you can get away. You don't merit acclaim.

11. You need to converse with your manager about a new occasion that is influencing the manner in which you and your colleagues play out your work. You:

A. Go about like you and your manager are closest friends, and request that she effectively fix the issue. All things considered, you could be managing everything comparably effectively as her, and you'd most likely improve.

B. Move toward the matter expertly and with certainty that an answer can be found. You propose any thoughts you could need to address the issue, and inquire as to whether she has any thoughts regarding what ought to be finished.

C. Could never attempt to converse with your chief. There's an explanation she is the chief and you're not. You could send her an unknown email or request one from your colleagues to converse with her.

12. This weekend you have 100 little ventures at home that must be handled, and you're feeling a piece overpowered. You:

A. Assault a few things immediately, beginning with the least demanding ones. You probably won't figure out how to complete any of them, yet you can constantly demand that another person contribute, in light of the fact that you have more significant activities.

B. Conclude which tasks should be finished first and take them on each in turn. By making things stride by step, you will complete what should be finished. If any other person is accessible at home, you'll request that they help out.

C. Weep over the lamentable spot of destiny that destroyed your end of the week. It's basically impossible that you'll at any point have the option to complete everything. You don't ask any other person for help since they have preferred activities over perform favours for you, and you would have zero desire to be an irritation.

13. The open door emerges for you to seek after the most amazing job you could ever imagine, yet it would mean leaving your current, stable position immediately. You:

A. Drop all that and pull out all the stops. Who needs a wellbeing net?

B. Gauge your choices, and plan out what you'll do assuming the new open door fails to work out. On the off chance that you have a mate, you examine the choice with them and make a contingency plan. In the event that it's conceivable, you'll figure out how to make it work.

C. Remain right where you are. Why risk frustration? You simply realize it won't end up actually working.

14. You have five minutes to get to an arrangement, and you're caught definitely having a tough time at a dead stop. You:

A. Revile, smoke, and blare your horn over and over. Don't these individuals acknowledge you're in a rush?

B. Are baffled, yet you realize there isn't a lot of you can do change what is happening. On the off chance that you have a cell, you call to tell them you will be somewhat late. You utilize the unforeseen chance to unwind and pay attention to your number one radio broadcast, or just to think.

C. Need to kick the bucket. Things like this generally appear to happen to you. It simply is absurd. You're so stressed over being late you're feeling wiped out, and it's basically impossible that you'll have the option to unwind until you're out of this wreck.

15. A colleague surveys one of your ventures and lets you know a couple of things that aren't charming, yet they are admirable sentiments. You:

A. Express gratitude toward him unwillingly, however demand that you understand what you're doing. In any case, he has a great deal of nerve scrutinizing your work, and his viewpoints don't exactly make any difference.

B. Are thankful for the chance to work on your work. You say thanks to him for his knowledge and revisit the task in view of his ideas prior to handing it over.

C. Surrender. You can do nothing right. Perhaps your associate ought to have been responsible for this undertaking rather than you. You'll simply hand it over and trust you don't get terminated for inadequacy.

Miserable Gus?

Results: Count up all your A, B, and C responses to find out where you rate on the confidence dipstick:

For the most part A:

Put Down That Mirror, Narcissus. Your tank overflowed. You may not know about it, yet you have definitely more certainty than you want. While certainty is a decent characteristic to have, a lot of it can cause you to seem haughty, inconsiderate or inaccessible. Attempt to take more notification of others' sentiments, and you'll get a lot further.

Or then again persevering blossom?

Generally B:

Join the Bazaar, You Have Amazing Equilibrium. You have a sound degree of confidence tempered with sympathy and worry for other people. You're likely the bubbling energy source everyone crowds around or the individual everybody comes to for help, and you're happy to give it when you can-however you know when you want time for yourself.

Generally C:

Assuming that You Dig Any More profound You'll Wind up in China. You're a couple of quarts low, and you could utilize a confidence top-off. You might figure you can do nothing right, yet with just enough self-assurance and some certain reasoning, you'll find you are worth undeniably more than you accept. In the event that you addressed C to everything, it's the ideal opportunity for a total framework flush and top off.

The Dim Ages: Adolescence Programming and Past Setbacks

"Upon our kids, how they are instructed, rests the destiny or fortune-of the upcoming scene."

- B. C. Forbes

The things we learn in youth aren't not difficult to forget-for the most part since we don't effectively recall them. Dislodging subliminal thought is far more earnestly. At the point when we are uninformed not just of why we embrace or keep away from specific things, yet in addition ignorant about the way that we are embracing or staying away from them, pinpointing the underlying foundations of our activities is a troublesome cycle.

Youth examples don't generally come from our folks, and frequently not even the messages we got from them were deliberately positioned there. For instance, assuming you guardians raised you to be useful, affable, considerate, and giving, you might have realized those examples so well that the general concept of working on something for yourself makes you wince and you may not know why. Then again, in the event that your folks gave you all that you needed without you truly looking for it or making the slightest effort, you might extend those equivalent assumptions on everybody around you-once more, with no thought why you're getting it done, or even that you are doing it by any stretch of the imagination. Ordinarily, obviously narrow minded individuals are stunned to find that others see them as childish. They might try and accept themselves the most thoughtful, most big-hearted individuals they know.

Another component you may not consider while attempting to get to your experience growing up writing computer programs is the external impacts that impacted your arrangement. Educators, childcare labourers or sitters, school companions, even irregular grown-ups in the supermarket might an affect your ways of behaving and convictions, whether deliberately or unwittingly.

However it could be difficult to decide all of your experience growing up impacts, you can provide yourself with an overall thought of previous occasions and characters that melded your ongoing convictions and do whatever it may take to transform them. The accompanying brief activity will assist you with getting everything rolling contemplating your triggers and propensities.

Work out: Interface the-impacts

1. Beginning with your folks, list the names of each and every individual you can review that you connected with during adolescence in a solitary segment down the left-hand side of a piece of paper. In the event that you don't have a clue about the name of an individual, utilize a short depiction, for example, "the woman toward the finish of the road with the noisy little canine." Incorporate family, companions, educators, parental figures, neighbours, and any other person you recall. On the off chance that you run out of room, tape one more piece of paper to the lower part of the first and continue onward down the left-hand side.

2. On the right-hand side of the paper, list every one of the propensities and attributes you have, both great and awful. Assuming you're feeling valiant, request that a companion assist you with concocting a portion of the characteristics you have that you probably won't know about. You don't for even a moment need to show anybody your rundown; you can hit them up and let them know you're getting an early advantage on your fresh new goals.

3. Presently comes the tomfoolery part. Attempt to coordinate each propensity or quality with one individuals from the left-hand section, and define a boundary to interface them. You might find that certain individuals have a few interfacing lines, while others have none.

Getting Back on the Pony

"Assuming that you have committed errors, even serious ones, there is generally one more opportunity for you. What we call disappointment isn't the tumbling down, however the remaining down."

- Mary Pickford

Past adolescence, you might have encountered mishaps or disappointments for which you obviously review the thinking. Frequently we are so against change that the smallest sign a better approach for doing things isn't working out turns into the sign to quit attempting. We are predictable animals, and thinking outside the box we've made for ourselves is a test not many feel they have the opportunity or the energy to confront.

Luckily, we can work on that shape until the breaks become wide to the point of breaking liberating. As per most therapists, it enjoys 21 days to reprieve a propensity. The activities and responses you foster because of setbacks are just propensities that you can free yourself of with training.

Your own reasoning might be "closing you in"!

Prepared for another activity? Make a rundown of the multitude of things you've attempted and quit doing prior to finishing (recollect, you haven't fizzled at them-you have just made an impermanent refuelling break on the way to progress). This rundown could incorporate weight control plans, goals, practice propensities, stopping smoking, or even self-improvement programs like this one. Leave yourself some space after everything. At the point when you get to the furthest limit of the rundown, return and fill in those propensities you have created as an outcome of standing by to see everything through to completion. For instance, assuming that you recorded "The Atkins Diet," your propensity may be "indulging on pasta since I didn't eat any for quite a long time." A portion of your propensities might be easy to change; others might require deviation from your planned course. In the pasta model, you could understand you can in any case eat pasta, only not as frequently as you have been while compensating for the misfortune. Concoct an option for each propensity that you can live with, so you don't short yourself before you get everything rolling. You could choose to have pasta two times per week rather than each and every other evening.

Since you have an aide, you can begin executing effective changes slowly and deliberately. Pick a couple of propensities you might want to change, and make certain to carry out the progressions every day for 21 days straight. It's useful to keep a diary or an outline to remind yourself what you're dealing with and why. You can likewise indulge yourself with a prize after the effective fulfilment of each propensity breaking cycle. What about a pleasant, enormous plate of spaghetti? Go on; you deserve it!

Back away from the Emergency signal: Overcoming Dread

"We all are brought into the world with a bunch of natural feelings of trepidation of falling, of the dim, of lobsters, of falling on lobsters in obscurity or talking before the Community Club, and of the words "Some Gathering Required."

- Dave Barry

Where all else neglects to prevent us from accomplishing what we need from life, dread strides in. We experience dread on both cognizant and oblivious levels, and it is quite possibly of the most restricting feeling we have. Now and again dread is legitimate, and, surprisingly, solid. For instance, an individual examining going across a bustling road will hold onto a solid feeling of dread toward being struck by two tons of quickly moving steel usually known as an engine vehicle (at any rate, on the off chance that the person in question is a sensibly normal individual who grasps the fundamental laws of physical science: moving vehicle + strolling individual = splat). This dread varieties alert, which makes the individual look left and right for cars moving the opposite direction and trust that a suitable time will wander across the street.

Notwithstanding, outlandish trepidation which can be similarly however devastating and sensible as legitimized dread seems to be all the more frequently the situation when dread is an element. Relatively few individuals put their lives in extreme danger consistently. Embarrassment, dismissal, and disappointment top the list of restricting feelings of trepidation that can be overwhelmed with training and assurance.

In reality, bugs top the rundown of fears for the vast majority. Arachnophobia-dread of bugs is the most well-known sort of dread on the planet. Be that as it may, feeling of dread toward bugs is totally reasonable, as insects are unpleasant eight-legged bugs with teeth, outsider eyes, and a propensity to dump on you all of a sudden.

One of the simplest and best techniques for managing dread is openness treatment, which is really confronting your feelings of trepidation each little move toward turn. On the off chance that you don't feel you can deal with openness treatment alone, enrol a companion to take part particularly on the off chance that you can find a companion who doesn't fear exactly the same things you do. With openness treatment, the goal is to encounter dread to a little degree a few times, so that each time it becomes simpler to prevail. (If it's not too much trouble, note that openness treatment doesn't matter to each circumstance. For instance, assuming you fear flying, it isn't suggested that you jump from progressively higher roosts and endeavour to become airborne.)

Here are a few different ways you can carry out openness treatment for the Huge Three feelings of dread:

Embarrassment

- Wear your shoes to the supermarket. In the event that you're feeling super bold, scrape your feet across the floor to point out your shoes. Assuming you're feeling super shy, go to a supermarket far enough from your home that the customers will presumably never see you from now onward.

- Sing at a karaoke bar. While you're clearheaded.

- Pick one totally improper piece of clothing (a Dr. Seuss cap, a major sets of fluffy gloves around mid-a headband with honey bee radio wire) and wear it in broad daylight as long as you can. This isn't just great openness treatment it's good times!

- Join a neighbourhood Speakers club or propose to give a public show on an area connecting with your skill at a library or school. Public talking is a superb channel for exorcizing embarrassment, particularly on the off chance that you do it consistently (that is talk in broad daylight, not embarrass yourself).

Dismissal

- Call up an emcee at a neighbourhood country radio broadcast and solicitation a melody by Metallica or Ozzy Osbourne. Know that you will be dismissed; you may be chuckled at and dismissed, and there is plausible you might be snickered at and dismissed on the air.

- In the event that you're single, utilize a web-based area administration like Classmates.com or PeopleFinder.com to find an outdated colleague you used to have eyes only for. Get in touch with them and request a date (or simply start a discussion). On the off chance that you're hitched, contact an outdated colleague and welcome them to lunch. Even from a pessimistic standpoint they'll say no, best case scenario, you will have rediscovered a companion.

- Compose a sonnet or a brief tale and attempt to submit it to a paper or magazine, or participate in a composing challenge. On the off chance that you're not dismissed, become an essayist right away.

Disappointment

- Attempt to nail Harden o to a tree.

- Purchase another computer game and endeavour to win it at a time. Assuming that you play computer games consistently, purchase a computer game that is not the same as the ones you generally play (for instance, on the off chance that you appreciate battling computer games, attempt a journey driven design. Or on the other hand video chess.).

- Begin another leisure activity that requires making a final result, for example, weaving, model unit building, or cake improving. Kindly note that assuming you are dealing with your dietary propensities, it isn't prudent to leave on cake-improving openness treatment to battle dread of disappointment. You will feel obliged to consume your bombed endeavours. All things considered, attempt vegetable model or natural product bowl plan.

- Challenge Jeff Gordon to a stock vehicle race. This will likewise assist with defeating your apprehensions about dismissal and embarrassment, as somewhere around one of them will undoubtedly occur.

Overcoming your feelings of dread resembles getting over a mountain - do it slowly and deliberately.

You can decide your own type of openness treatment by thinking of ways of confronting your own feelings of trepidation each little move toward turn. On the off chance that you can't imagine anything, request that a companion help. A great many people are eager to take a stab at a novel, new thing, particularly on the off chance that they get to watch you accomplish something engaging.

These activities are not expected as a substitute for proficient mental consideration. In the event that your feelings of trepidation are major areas of strength for remarkably impede typical capabilities or day to day exercises, you ought to look for the counsel of an ensured specialist. Self-prompted openness treatment can be powerful in lessening or easing typical trepidation, yet ought not be utilized in instances of intellectually devastating or injury actuated dread.

Injury: Breaking the Chains

"In the event that you're going through some serious hardship, continue onward."

- Sir Winston Churchill

Awful things happen to great individuals. It's an unavoidable truth. Quite possibly of the most unprecedented thing about people is our ability for strength notwithstanding injury. Marvellous endurance and recuperation are not periodic happenings on the planet. Consistently, somebody endures a misfortune. Consistently, somebody moves toward a more joyful life in spite of a past injury. Consistently, life goes on, and we change. Also, we are more grounded for it.

The ideas in this part, by and by, are not substitutes for proficient mental consideration. In any case, many individuals have found self-improvement compelling for freeing the pressure from injury and assuming command over themselves. Whether you decide to look for proficient assistance or set out on a mending way yourself, realize that you can break free and start to live again when misfortune contacts you. You don't need to allow injury to hold you back from accomplishing what you truly desire.

You can pick only one, or any mix of these procedures to deal with liberating yourself from injury. On the off chance that you are awkward with a methodology, continue on toward another determination.

"It very well may Be More regrettable": Performance and Mindfulness

For gentle injury, now and again giggling truly is the best medication. Assuming you can take a gander at the circumstance equitably, you might have the option to "dismiss it," or possibly arm yourself with enough information to acknowledge you had it simple.

There are two methods for moving toward this strategy. The first is to utilize your creative mind basically. Picture the injury, and afterward envision every one of the manners by which it might have been more regrettable.

The second way to deal with performance and attention to minor injury is to explore genuine situations where the circumstances of others ended up being more regrettable than yours. You can look online for reports, or peruse the periodicals file at your nearby library. For the most part, you can continuously find cases concerning individuals who had more trouble than you, at this point they made due and you will as well. All things considered, you're as yet alive. To make this technique a stride further, you can effectively help other people in your circumstance. Make a gift to a particular case or a connected foundation, or begin a help program or asset drive locally. Making a move, regardless of how little, frequently assists with easing the sensations of misfortune and vulnerability related with injury.

For Your Eyes As it were: Journaling to Delivery

Keeping a diary or journal is perhaps of humanity's most seasoned custom. The contemplations, sentiments and feelings of ages have been safeguarded through endless pages engraved with words that are in many cases kept hidden over the lifetime of the essayist, and uncovered exclusively in light of a legitimate concern for adding to verifiable record.

For remedial purposes, at times the actual demonstration of recording past injury permits you to confront it all the more completely and discharge the pessimistic sentiments related with the occasion. The journaling system can be a transient program utilized exclusively for dealing with a particular injury. On the off chance that you keep a transient diary, you might wish to consume or obliterate it toward the finish of the cycle as a representative acknowledgment of your independence from injury. In the event that you appreciate journaling, you might wish to keep keeping a set up account of your viewpoints and sentiments. Many individuals keep every day or week by week diaries their whole lives. Journaling is a brilliant type of self-correspondence that can help you whether you've encountered injury in your life.

There are a wide range of configurations your diary can take. Following are probably the most widely recognized, yet go ahead and think of your own journaling style to suit your particular requirements:

- Freestyle thought. Freestyle composing is a method utilized by many creators and hopeful creators to kick off innovativeness. Keeping a freestyle diary is an effective method for uncovering considerations you might be concealing even from yourself, and for fledglings it's a fantastic beginning stage. The guidelines for composing freestyle are straightforward: simply plunk down with your diary and composing carry out of decision, and begin composing. Try not to stress over spelling, language, or even cognizance. Basically record whatever rings a bell. Attempt to do this for something like five minutes to give your psychological motors time to heat up. In the event that you don't want to stop following five minutes, simply continue to compose. Day to day freestyle composing is one of the most remedial practices that anyone could hope to find.

- Memory discharge. This method is generally valuable for present moment journaling, especially in the event that you plan to obliterate the diary in an emblematic way when you're done. Memory discharge journaling is precisely exact thing it seems like: you just record your recollections of injury and any sentiments related with them, and afterward discharge those gloomy sentiments. Envision that they are currently on paper, and subsequently as of now not in your heart or brain. Consequently, it is more compelling to annihilate the diary when you are done with it.

- Dear Jerk letters. If a particular individual or gathering, living or dead, was answerable for the injury in your life, composing a letter or series of letters to them can be useful in rising above your injury. You won't most likely ever send them the letters, however placing down in actual structure what you would agree to them in the event that you could is gigantically fulfilling on an individual level. You can address the letters to their names, or give them inventive monikers (Dear Jerk, Dear Companion Stealer, Dear Rubbish of the Earth) to safeguard your protection and add more kick to your searing talks.

- Story-structure treatment. A few injuries are excessively new or excessively excruciating to completely remember. In these cases, composing a fictionalized record of the experience can be useful in delivering gloomy feelings. You can change the names, areas, ages, or even sexes of the members in your own injury to provide yourself with a more goal perspective on the circumstance and help you in adapting or tracking down conclusion. Making substitute renditions of the circumstance assists with dislodging terrible sentiments. You might keep in touch with yourself a blissful consummation, or give your imaginary self-triumph over your oppressor.

- Pictorial diaries. You might feel words are deficient to convey your horrendous feelings. If so, you should seriously mull over drawing a diary all things considered. Similarly as you don't need to be a decent essayist to keep a diary, you don't need to be a decent craftsman to draw one. Utilize anything that structure you feel alright with, whether it is stick figures, theoretical jotting, or completely nitty gritty delivering. The main significant stage in journaling is to write something substantial down, and nobody yet you will at any point need to check it out.

Picking the right diary can be similarly basically as significant as what you place inside it. The human psyche is something strong, and our considerations and discernments impact our activities. The following are a couple of tips on picking a fitting diary for your independent treatment:

- The size, design, look and feel of your diary ought to be emblematic, both of your expectations or your character. Take as much time as is needed in selecting a diary you appreciate checking out and holding. Allow yourself to spend somewhat more than you generally would, and stay away from deals or deals (except if the one at a bargain is precisely exact thing you're searching for). Connecting a marginally higher dollar worth to your diary than what you could pay for something like a regular school-grade winding scratch pad gives the significance of your diary a psychological lift, and advises you that what you put inside it means quite a bit to you. In the event that you don't need any other person to peruse your diary, come what may, put resources into one with a lock.

- Pick a composing carry out that you will utilize explicitly for your diary. Except for a pictorial diary, pencil is the most unfortunate medium to use, as it conveys the feeling of a transitory express that can be changed with a pass of the eraser. Pen or marker are the most ideal decisions. You ought to compose with the medium you feel most good in, that benefits you in a representative or critical manner. You can pick an ink variety you like, purchase a bunch of sparkle pens, get a curiosity pen, or even get a dated plume pen-they are accessible in ballpoint renditions or conventional etch point and inkwell styles. Make certain to just utilize the composing execute you decide for your diary, and not for staple records or writing down telephone numbers.

- Find a permanent spot for your diary and keep it there except if you're writing in it. Laying out a long-lasting spot for your diary under the bed, on the first rate in the storeroom, in a bureau compartment, on your end table is a significant stage in your journaling schedule. This assists with building up lastingness and structure new propensities (and takes out the chance of losing your diary).

Reflection: Interfacing Above Torment

Reflection is a respected unwinding strategy that has been utilized effectively in Eastern societies for quite a long time to reduce pressure and centre the psyche. This method has as of late acquired prominence in the US as a large number of individuals find both the physical and psychological wellness advantages of contemplation, while understanding that it's not quite as troublesome as it sounds.

In injury applications, contemplation can assist you with revamping the energy your pessimistic feelings destroy and figure out how to adapt to the challenges related with injury. Contemplation is one of the simplest and most cheap types of self-treatment: all you want is yourself and a peaceful room.

There are a few varieties of contemplation you can perform. You ought to pick the means or mix of steps you're generally OK with and use them consistently. Following are an only a couple of the many contemplation structures in presence; or you can join components of various reflection projects to make your own special technique.

In all strategies for reflection, the article is to get your psyche free from cognizant idea and focus on essentially existing at the time.

Strolling Reflection: When you perform strolling contemplation, you can think and exercise simultaneously. To ponder while strolling, you just focus on either the sensation of your foot meeting the earth with each step, or on your breathing, which ought to be loose and normal. Accomplishing focus to shut out thought takes practice, yet the regular cadence of strolling gives an incredible beginning stage to the starting contemplation understudy.

Standing Contemplation: Performing standing reflection is an effective method for rehearsing legitimate breathing, as a standing position is helpful for right stance and completely open aviation routes. To work on standing contemplation, stand straight and easily with your feet pointed forward, roughly a mid-length separated. Place your hands one over the other on your lower mid-region and focus on relaxing. Take slow breaths and hold for around four seconds prior to delivering gradually. Appropriate reflection breathing is finished through the nose, both in and out. Standing reflection can be performed with your eyes open or shut, as indicated by your inclination.

Situated Contemplation: This is the most famous type of reflection. In a peaceful room, be situated either in an agreeable seat with your feet level on the floor, or on the floor in a leg over leg position (generally Indian or Lotus). Likewise with standing contemplation, you can focus on breathing and gradually void your brain of thought. Situated reflection is performed with loose, open eyes zeroed in on a decent point on the floor roughly three feet before you. A huge number of situated contemplation utilize outer improvements for focus (see "Reflection with Outside Boost).

Drop That Horseshoe: Misfortune can't really exist

"Rely upon the hare's foot maybe, yet recall it didn't work for the bunny."

- R. E. Shay

Have you broken a mirror in the beyond seven years? Any dark felines crossed your way recently? In essentially every culture, in all aspects of the world, there are a few things credited to karma: the opportunity occurring of fortunate or unfortunate occasions, otherwise called fortune or destiny. Karma is utilized as the defence for quite a few apparently incomprehensible conditions. A player winning a large number of games at a gambling club table is supposed to be "riding a fortunate streak" (however his rewards can probably be credited to some extent to some extent to expertise); a vagrant is considered "doing pretty bad" (however there is more than likely a substantial, though sad, situation behind his unfortunate express); a person for whom things generally appear to go ok is attributed "the karma of the Irish" (and exactly what, supplicate tell, is so fortunate about Ireland?).

The people who buy into the karma hypothesis and notice strange notions, for example, staying away from the number 13 and throwing salt over the left shoulder when it spills will demand that it works. As far as they might be concerned, it takes care of business; be that as it may, this is just a demonstration of the force of the psyche to convince us to see what we wish to see. Karma works similarly as sure reasoning. Assuming you accept you are "protected" in light of the fact that you try not to open umbrellas in the house and strolling under stepping stools, then you will be protected. Then again, on the off chance that you break a mirror and persuade yourself that misfortune is bound to contaminate you, you will subliminally damage yourself and thusly draw in misfortune or at any rate, chalk up lamentable occasions to the breaking of the mirror as opposed to finding what truly occurred so you can forestall a reoccurrence of the issue. Seven years is quite a while to trust that your karma will change.

It's your time - how might you spend it?

Rather than scouring the guts of pregnant ladies or expecting to find heads-up pennies lying around, why not attempt positive reasoning? You will accomplish similar outcomes, and you will not need to depend on finding good luck charms or try not to step on walkway breaks. Utilizing the force of positive reasoning is as straightforward as possible and will happen to you. You don't need to retain a muddled arrangement of rules or keep elaborate customs to draw in satisfaction and achievement. So throw that fortunate tee shirt from secondary school and tap in to positive reasoning today. Your misfortune sentence is formally released.

Alter Your Perspective, Completely change you

"Most people are comparably blissful as they make up their brains to be."

- Abraham Lincoln

While tapping in to the force of positive reasoning, the main step is to make a mentality that permits you to emphatically think. Whenever you have pulled the weeds from your psychological nursery, you can start to plant the seeds that will secure your better approach for life.

Making a positive mentality takes preparing. In much similar way as sprinters train their bodies to get through extensive stretches of supported action, you can prepare your psyche to support positive idea, and normally concede to charming or hopeful ways. Right away, thinking emphatically may feel abnormal or crazy (especially assuming you're the sort of individual who accepts energetic morning individuals ought to be shot). Remember, however, that it gets simpler the more you make it happen, and at last, supporting a positive outlook will be pretty much as normal as relaxing.

Like any preparation program, there are steps you can follow to accomplish your ideal outcomes: for this situation, a positive mental viewpoint. You might review that it requires 21 days to shape another propensity (what's that...you've failed to remember as of now? Return and add "long haul memory" to your rundown of propensities you might want to get to the next level). Subsequently, you ought to play out every one of the means for somewhere around 21 back to back days. You can approach on slowly and carefully, or execute the entire program; simply be certain you're not forgetting about anything.

Move forward to your psychological treadmill, and let the preparation start!

Warm-up: Shake Out Regrettable Wrinkles

At the point when you consider it, it's self-evident: negative is something contrary to positive, so to impart a positive mentality you really want to dispose of negative contemplations. Sounds adequately straightforward, correct? The interaction is a simple one, yet it takes practice to make it stick.

The most important phase in cleaning pessimism off of your brain is to focus on your viewpoints, as a matter of fact. Whenever the words can't, shouldn't, wouldn't, will not, not, or never occur to you, focus on the thing you're thinking and turn it around to dispose of the negative phrasing. For instance:

Your mate and kids are away for a couple of hours, and you have the spot to yourself. You're enjoying one of your #1 exercises. Amidst your pleasure, you begin to feel remorseful. You think: I truly ought not to be doing this. I could be getting everything rolling on the undertaking I guaranteed another person I'd deal with. Your delight begins to blur, and you stop what you're doing, angry that you need to handle this exhausting task when you have so brief period to yourself...

Does this sound natural? The second you hear yourself think shouldn't, stop not too far off and head in a different path. In this situation, you could rather think I truly ought to do this. Getting some margin for me is significant, and when I'm loose and fulfilled I will actually want to improve on that project I guaranteed another person. I'm so happy I got the chance to accomplish something I appreciate.

Attempt to do this each time a negative idea creeps in. The more frequently you oust negative thoughts from your brain, the simpler positive reasoning will turn into. You will be more loose and responsive to positive arrangements.

Work Those Mouth Muscles

In the event that words generally can't do a picture justice, a grin merits 1,000,000. The force of a grin is inconceivable. Regardless of whether you want to grin, the straightforward demonstration of lifting the edges of your mouth can assist you with lifting your whole soul and find something that would merit grinning about. Probably the best self-improvement exhortation out there comes from the individuals who advocate "counterfeit it until you make it." This is particularly evident with regards to positive reasoning, and faking a grin goes far toward creating the certifiable thing. You might wind up snickering at yourself only on the grounds that you realize you don't have anything to grin about.

One more incredible thing about grins they're profoundly infectious. A grin spreads quicker than a chilly in a childcare. The vast majority can't resist the urge to grin back when somebody projects a blissful articulation their way. This is a basic and invigorating hypothesis that you can try out for yourself. Go to any open spot and begin grinning indiscriminately individuals, then monitor the number of grin back (even dubious sneering counts!). You'll probably find that 9 out of 10 of your objectives return your upbeat articulation to some little degree, and you've likely quite recently filled their heart with joy somewhat more brilliant, as well.

Figuring out how to look favourably upon request is a significant stage in fostering a forever sure mentality. One great strategy for calling grins is to pick a blissful memory that never neglects to fill you with positive sentiments. Keep this memory at the front of your psychological inventory, and access it at whatever point you feel an instance of the blues coming on. It may not tackle your concerns, yet it will basically make you grin which thus helps you unwind and investigate what is happening. Grinning frequently makes a psychological signal for the groundwork of positive reasoning and helps prepare of satisfaction.

You ought to likewise invest a little energy before the mirror noticing your own demeanours. At first this training might appear to be awkward or tremendously senseless, however grinning at your own appearance emphatically affects your mind. You might actually rehearse different grin varieties: the entertained sneer; the quiet leg-pulling grin; the excited smile; the laugh uncontrollably surprised grin. Consider it an Olympic event...it's your own Grin Long distance race, and you'll win the gold without fail!

Do A few Reps

While fostering a positive outlook, the significance of reiteration can't be put into words. Practice is the way to building any muscle, so by review your hopeful standpoint as a muscle, you can foster a hold of bliss that will bring you through the most overwhelming occasions.

This isn't to say you shouldn't stress over anything. Disregarding alarming occasions won't make them disappear. Dealing with your concerns while taking a gander at them through a positive lens is significant. The positive attitude itself doesn't delete your difficulties. It is basically an instrument to permit you to find an answer without wearing yourself out through pressure and tension. You will track down it far more straightforward to take care of issues when you can step back and take a gander at the circumstance in a positive light; and frequently the arrangement will introduce itself with little exertion, just on the grounds that your psyche is clear and open to the point of seeing it.

The more you practice positive reasoning, the more normally it will come to you. You will find that baffling regular events wane to minor aggravations, and in the end quit upsetting you by and large. Continue to rehearse positive perspectives, and you will be well headed to a low-stress, high-energy way of life that will permit you to achieve anything you want.

A fantastic accomplishment - rehearsed and imagined multiple times.

Cool-Down: Feel the Consume

As you arrive at the finish of your everyday positive reasoning exercise, think back and consider your advancement. Was there whatever appeared to be more straightforward to you? Is it true that you were ready to find a quicker answer for an issue that could have conventionally gobbled up a great deal of time in stressing? Do you feel more loose and prepared to attempt once more tomorrow?

Salute yourself on your triumphs. By supporting your achievements, you help to firm the underpinning of your new certain attitude and lay the foundation for your prosperity.

Exchanging Terminals: Connect to Positive Energy

"No doubter at any point found the mystery of the stars, or cruised to an unfamiliar land, or opened another entryway for the human soul."

- Helen Keller

Energy is the daylight of your psyche's nursery. Having energy for all that you do is fundamental for the course of positive reasoning. Similarly as plants expect daylight to create and develop, using the force of positive reasoning expects excitement to empower your true capacity and guarantee a perpetual stockpile of fuel.

You will find that the more excitement you create, the more energy you'll need to place in. There are a few things it will be not difficult to produce excitement over, and others where you'll need to extend yourself to find what will start your pleasure. For instance, nobody experiences difficulty producing excitement for spending a surprising reward from work or requiring an evening out on the town. Be that as it may, you might find it hard to become amped up for cleaning dishes or finishing up your personal tax documents. In any case, part of the enchantment of positive reasoning is fostering the capacity to track down the beneficial things in any circumstance and use them to get past the troublesome aspects.

Like fostering a positive outlook, energy should be developed and shielded from possibly harming profound tempests. There are a few strategies you can use to place a portion of energy into all that you do, whether at long last taking dream get-away or cleaning out the cellar. You can pick the technique that best fits anything circumstance you're confronting and guarantee yourself the energy to handle everything life ends up concocting.

How might this benefit me?

One of the most basic answers for finding energy is to zero in on the advantage you will get from following through with a specific job. In certain circumstances finding the benefit is simple. For example, you might abhor wrapping presents, however you realize the individual you're giving the present to will be excited when given this exquisite paper-wrapped gift, thus you get joy from imagining the beneficiary opening the present. This is a particularly valuable strategy when you're still up at 2 a.m. on Christmas early daytime attempting to sort out some way to wrap the bike you've quite recently endured three hours assembling.

Different conditions won't have such clear advantages. If you somehow happened to end up attempting to change a punctured tire out and about in the centre of a blizzard (or a rainstorm, in the event that you are sufficiently lucky to live in a without snow environment) it would without a doubt be challenging to track down your silver lining. Under unpleasant conditions, allow yourself to consider the most stunning advantage you can think of. Maybe you were en route to a party you would prefer not to have gone to. All things considered, your punctured tire would give you the ideal reason to pivot and return home.

There is what is happening, whether it's as an advantage or an example to be learned (Illustration One: Never drive with problematic tires through a blizzard to a party you would have rather not gone to in the first positioned). You can tackle the force of positive reasoning by finding that great and taking advantage of it, regardless of how little or inconsequential it might appear.

The Pal Framework

In the event that you're experiencing difficulty bringing energy for a specific undertaking, attempt to search out somebody who appreciates doing something like that and request that they accomplice up with you. Like grinning, excitement is infectious. Assuming you invest some energy noticing someone else's excitement, some of coming off on you is bound.

In the event that you don't know anybody who may be excited about the thing you're attempting to achieve, take a stab at going on the web to look into articles or sites (web logs, which are generally private, routinely refreshed web-based diaries) relating to the subject. Once in a while simply learning about another person's energy can assist you with discovering a part of the undertaking to appreciate, and help you through it with a negligible measure of pressure, nervousness and fear. (Be cautioned: it could be challenging to find anybody who appreciates scouring latrines or discharging feline litter boxes. In these cases, you may be all alone!)

Information is Power

Wading through a specific errand or project can be overwhelming on the off chance that you don't have any idea what you're doing. Assuming you're the kind of individual who never requests headings or peruses the directions, you might be enticed to take on difficulties in regions where your insight is restricted. Regardless of whether you're not, you might wind up confronted with taking on an undertaking you don't feel able to deal with, whether it's filling in for somebody in an alternate division at work or changing a baby's diaper interestingly.

The more you realize about the thing you're doing, the simpler it will be to achieve. This might appear to be obvious, yet many individuals don't understand that you can constantly figure out more data. It just requires a couple of moments to look into something on the web, counsel a reference book, or hit up somebody you know has insight with the issue you're confronting.

Acquiring information has different advantages too. The more you realize about a given subject, the better you will actually want to zero in on your objective and work toward it. You can't arrive at your objective on the off chance that you can't track down the way. View information as the pruning shears of your psychological nursery, making room for excitement to develop and spread. With the right arrangement of apparatuses, you can achieve any errand without any problem.

Make all necessary endorsements

Being focused on accomplishing your point is fundamental to producing a feeling of energy. Whether you need to have shining white teeth or glimmer your silvery whites at hordes of thousands as you acknowledge your Institute Grant, you ought to be totally dedicated to what you're attempting to achieve.

One method for establishing your own responsibility is to frame a bit by bit plan for arriving at your objectives. You can do this with any undertaking, regardless of how incredible or little (however you could save time to create a psychological arrangement for things like washing the supper dishes, as it could require you more investment to record everything than it would to wash them as a matter of fact). On a piece of paper-or for fantastic errands like evolving professions, toward the start of a scratch pad note your beginning stage: where you are presently. Leave yourself some space, and afterward write down where you need to be and the way in which long you anticipate taking to arrive. Then return and separate the most common way of getting from point A to point B in nitty gritty advances. This not just assists you with envisioning arriving at your objective, it additionally permits you to check ventures off as you complete them. Your excitement will be supported as you move more toward your objective.

While you're getting things on paper, consider making an agreement with yourself to arrive at your goal. You might in fact ask a companion or relative to go about as an observer, which will additionally set your expectations to see everything through to completion. Your agreement can be a straightforward report expressing your guarantee to yourself, or an itemized guide of the things you will do to assist yourself with arriving at your points, with cut-off time dates for extra inspiration and eruptions of energy. Update your agreement as often as possible noticeably to help yourself to remember your goals. Each time you see it, you will get yourself anxious to accomplish your objective and satisfy your agreement.

Hang Your Own Carrot

Ask any entrepreneur and you'll figure out that prizes are perhaps of the most impressive inspiration. Individuals are more able to pursue an objective when they realize they will receive something in return toward the end. Since your supervisor most likely won't compensate you for getting more fit or redesigning your washroom, you can want to give yourself a prize when you meet a given objective.

While choosing self-rewards, make certain to match them to your objectives. This won't just guarantee you don't become weary of a similar prize, yet will likewise help you while you're arranging the procedures you'll use to achieve your points. For instance, in the event that you might want to invest less energy staring at the TV and additional time outside or with your family, you can compensate yourself with an excursion to the theatre to see an extraordinary film. On the off chance that you're intending to stop smoking, a piece of your procedure could be to save a portion of the cash you'll save by not accepting cigarettes and get yourself another outfit, or something you've had your eye on for some time however haven't had the option to manage.

A few objectives accompany natural rewards previously inherent, yours for the guaranteeing when you arrive at your goal. For instance, assuming that you will go into business, you definitely realize you'll be compensated by working independently, potentially even by working out of your home. Whether you're working for a natural prize or furnishing yourself with a motivation, treating yourself is an incredible method for producing excitement for the job that needs to be done.

Give up

Truth be told. Some of the time, you ought to simply surrender.

This may not be the kind of counsel you'd hope to track down in a book about certain reasoning. Nonetheless, there is a particular time when you ought to give up and that is the point at which you disdain doing what you're doing.

"Like what you do. In the event that you could do without it, accomplish something different."

- Paul Harvey

Such a large number of individuals wind up making due with the existence they figure they should have, the existence others have advised them to expect, or the existence they accept they're left with. You should understand that there is room on this planet for everybody, and in the event that you're feeling caught in a task you scorn or a living space you can't stand, you really want to roll out an improvement not too far off, when you have time, or when you get anything that it is you've been sitting tight for; yet at the present time. That subtle "sometime in the not so distant future" is continuously going to be from here on out, and you can't get up to speed to what's in store. This present time is the main opportunity you have.

This doesn't mean you ought to drop all that and laugh in the face of any potential risk at any rate, not by and large. Assuming you're similar to a great many people, you have liabilities that should be dealt with.

SHOOTS AND LEAVES

"Inspiration kicks you off. Moves you along propensity."

- Jim Ryan

Now that you've established your psychological nursery, you will begin to see the starting points of development in yourself and your environmental elements. At this stage, sustaining the delicate fresh starts of your sure, positive self is significant. You ought to figure out how to perceive the impacts of positive reasoning in your life and support the advancement of solid roots to secure yourself in progress.

Determination makes a difference.

The Primary Indications of Your Spring of Resurrection

"There's just a single corner of the universe you can be sure of improving, and that is your own self."

- Aldous Huxley

As you work on utilizing positive reasoning, you will find that things start to change for you. In some cases the change is so continuous you notice nothing by any stretch of the imagination, until one day another person lets you know that you appear to be changed. They might inquire as to whether you've gotten another outfit, changed your hair, shed pounds, or walked away with that sweepstakes. Tapping in to positive reasoning not just makes you more joyful, it additionally makes you more alluring; the sort of individual others need to be near.

Now that you've had some insight, you could perceive a portion of the normal indications of decidedly charged individuals. Look at this rundown of things you need to anticipate.

You know you're a Positive Mastermind When:

- Your exhausting drive to work goes by so rapidly, you can't help thinking about why it at any point irritated you in any case.
- The representative at the supermarket gives you some unacceptable change, you bring up it cheerfully and she joyfully amends the slip-up.
- You held up in line at the bank for 25 minutes on your lunch hour...and your life didn't end.
- The new part for your vehicle at long last shown up at the carport following seven days on delay purchase, yet it was some unacceptable one. You were so decent about tolerating the deferral when the carport called that they offered you a significant markdown on your maintenance bill.
- Each time you get a brief look at yourself in a mirror, you're grinning and you don't think you seem to be an idiot.
- You put the stove on too high and consumed dinner...then wound having something far superior to you'd arranged.
- Out of nowhere you have much more leisure time on your hands, and a lot of activities with it-in addition to enough energy to do them.
- The last time you figured the word can't was in the expression I can't completely accept that this multitude of extraordinary things are occurring to me.

Positive reasoning has the ability to transform you, as long as you accept it does. As you keep on utilizing positive reasoning strategies, you will find you don't need to invest a lot of energy into accomplishing what you need.

Paranoid notion: The Greatest Danger to the Upgraded You

"Whenever a man focuses a finger at another person, he ought to recall that four of his fingers are pointing at himself."

- Louis Nizer

Each way has its obstructions. Along the way to positive reasoning, you will see as only one: yourself. People tend to make connivances against themselves and force oneself restricting convictions that encompass them on each part of their lives, whether these prohibitive beliefs result from climate, childhood, or a blend of persuasive variables.

You may not actually perceive your own foolish activities. In any case, the ability to get to the advantages of positive reasoning rests exclusively inside yourself-and you are the one in particular that can hinder you. Hence, you should figure out how to move to one side and permit yourself to create to your maximum capacity.

Following are the absolute most normal examples of self-restricting way of behaving, alongside steps you can remove to get from your own specific manner and burst your own way to joy and achievement.

There's in every case tomorrow: Annihilate Stalling

"To be continuously expecting to make a new and better life however never carve out opportunity to set about it is as... to put off eating and drinking and dozing over time until you're dead."

-Og Mandino

Hesitation is the simplest thing on the planet to awesome and one of the hardest propensities to break. There will constantly be a valid justification to put off anything you desire to achieve, whether it's vacuuming the parlour cover or at long last taking that European get-away you've been making arrangements for years.

At the point when you understand you're putting something off, quite possibly of everything thing you can manage is to wonder why you would rather not make it happen. The explanations behind tarrying are essentially as shifted as individuals who practice it: the undertaking is exhausting or dull; you are apprehensive you will not have the option to deal with it; the venture is troublesome or tedious; it will be an undesirable encounter; you fear the potential outcomes of owning the errand to the end. When you realize what is preventing you from pushing forward, you can decide your methodology for achieving your objective and stall un-out.

How would you pulverize tarrying in its tracks? The solutions for moving past hesitation include:

- Take care of business. Anything that the undertaking you're confronting, basically pick a point and begin. Frequently things are not quite as awful as they appear, and when you begin doing something it's simpler to gather speed that will bring you all the way to completion. Let yourself know that when you complete the unsavoury responsibility, you will not make them loom over your head and you can continue on toward better things.

• Split it up, individuals. Require a couple of moments to separate bigger undertakings into little, sensible objectives. For instance, assuming that you are endeavouring to sort out your work area at work, you could pick one cabinet and finish that, and afterward have some time off and accomplish something different prior to returning for the following cabinet. Meeting a progression of little objectives is more spurring and empowering than attempting to handle an immense undertaking at the same time.

• Slice through the puff. Set yourself up to deal with interruptions while you're taking on an undertaking. If conceivable, overlook the telephone and certainly oppose the compulsion to play Solitaire or check your email multiple times. Ensure your psyche is made up to do anything that it is you're doing and nothing else until it's done. You will feel better realizing it's finished, and you'll squander less life on side-line projects.

• Adhere to the program. Guarantee you have sufficient opportunity to follow through with the responsibility you're beginning. Assuming you realize you will be intruded on or used up all available time before you're through, pick one piece of the errand to finish as opposed to attempting to race through the entire thing. Hurrying to fulfil a time constraint you realize you can't make causes more pressure, and can really get things going more slow in light of the fact that you're stressed that you will not have the option to achieve what you've decided to do. Offer yourself a reprieve, and your anxiety will much obliged.

• Look for something incredible. Regardless of our best sure reasoning endeavours, things really do sometimes take a turn for the unforeseen. Delays are a given much of the time. While you're arranging an errand or objective, it is critical to figure time in the event that things turn out badly. Delays are a significant facilitator of tarrying: it's not difficult to persuade yourself to put things off when you as of now need to stand by. Ensure you have a plan B set up so you can try not to put things off regardless meet your consummation objectives serenely.

Simply Say No: How not to take on something over the top

"The best chief is the person who has sense to the point of picking great men to do what he needs finished, and poise to the point of holding back from interfering with them while they make it happen."

- Theodore Roosevelt

Individuals are continuously going to request that you get things done for them. Such is reality. Frequently we are approached to commit to responsibilities we feel really awkward with, lack the capacity to deal with, or downright don't have any desire to make-however saying "no" aggravates us than consenting to something we could do without.

Ladies particularly succumb to the over-responsibility disorder. You ought to regularly practice it to say "no" more regularly, especially when you know that consenting to take on a specific responsibility will unleash ruin with your life, despite the fact that the little voice in your mind is telling you tolerating would be the "decent" what should be done. With regards to your mental soundness, the most pleasant thing is to ensure you don't overstretch yourself and wind up playing out an enormous number of errands with unsatisfactory outcomes.

You can indeed fit a limited amount a lot of through that entryway!

The most important phase in figuring out how to say no is concluding which things you ought to consent to focus on, and which things are good to pass on. This choice ought to come from your own needs; the things that are mean a lot to you and your life. This is one motivation behind why it's essential to characterize your objectives plainly when you start utilizing the force of positive reasoning. Gauge each solicitation against your objectives and conclude whether consenting to them would draw you nearer or further away from your targets.

At the point when you get to a place where you should decline a solicitation, there are multiple ways of expressing no without making feel terrible or causing yourself to seem discourteous. Be basically as legitimate as conceivable while saying no, and you will actually want to continue with an irreproachable inner voice.

Need a reason? Here are the main ten methods for saying no pleasantly:

1. "No." Occasionally, the most effective way to decline is graciously, however straightforwardly. On the off chance that somebody in your life is continually requesting that you do things they could without much of a stretch handle themselves, a firm "no" is the best way to inspire them to stop. One more way to deal with hazardous individuals with successive solicitations is to tell them, "I realize you'll work effectively taking care of it all alone."

2. "I'm in a few different ventures/responsibilities this moment." Don't hesitate for even a moment to let individuals know when you're occupied. Most will regard your timetable and track down one more method for satisfying their solicitations for help. You ought not to be supposed to drop assignments you've proactively focused on to finish new ones.

3. "I want to zero in on [my profession, my family, my own life] right now." Assuming you're going through a troublesome time in one more part of your life that requires your consideration, make it a point to taking on additional solicitations. You don't be guaranteed to need to make sense of your particular thinking for taking a pass; simply show that you

4. "I don't feel I'm the best individual to deal with that assignment." When you don't feel able to deal with something mentioned of you, say as much. Make sense of that you would rather not make a lacklustre display, since you realize this errand is essential to the individual

requesting that you make it happen. Chances are, they need the assignment gotten along nicely, as well.

5. "I can't make it happen, however I know another person who can." Just utilize this "no" structure on the off chance that you genuinely know somebody who can deal with the undertaking, has opportunity and energy to make it happen. It's ideal to have the option to offer elective assistance, yet provided that you can finish your proposition. Alluding individuals to another person who will not have the option to help either will be seen as a get over; the individual who initially came to you won't think you ever really needed to help them in any case.

6. "I'm not happy/despise doing that." Stay consistent. Assuming that you're approached to accomplish something that appears to be off-base or an undertaking you loathe doing, don't consent to it and make sense of why. This way you will actually want to keep away from rehash demands for exactly the same thing.

7. "I can't assist with correcting now, however ask me later." Once more, be straightforward with this assertion. To assist, yet don't have the opportunity when the solicitation is made, let the individual asking you know that you'd be eager to assist out when you can. On the off chance that conceivable, give them a particular accessibility, similar to tomorrow or one week from now, when you realize you'll be free. In the event that they need the assignment done previously, they will find another person.

8. "I have no involvement in this kind of errand." This is like expressing you're not the most obviously qualified individual, huger basically for you. At the point when you take on an undertaking for another person, you shouldn't need to get familiar with an entirely different range of abilities just to finish a certain something. In any case, in the event that it's something you were wanting to advance at any rate, you should make the most of the chance to gain some new useful knowledge.

9. "I realize you need to [other individual's objective] however I can't move away from [other commitment] the present moment." This is a pleasant method for recognizing the necessities of the other individual while declining to overburden yourself. This can likewise open the chance to deal with the foundational problem of the solicitation in a manner that is helpful for both of you.

10. "No, but..." If for reasons unknown you can't focus on a solicitation, you can offer an elective that would be gainful to the circumstance. Maybe you can't play out the particular errand mentioned, however there is one more part of the venture you would have the option to assist with. Once more, this leaves your choices open without causing you to appear to be unfeeling or uninterested with whomever is making a solicitation of you.

Work on saying no both at home and at work, at whatever point you're approached to bite off you realize you can chew. Overstretching yourself can be a hard propensity to break, however it is a fundamental stage in escaping your own particular manner so you can achieve your life's objectives. You merit time for yourself, and you should be answerable for guaranteeing your own necessities are met.

Accept Me As I'm: Kicking the Endorsement Propensity

"You can't be desolate in the event that you like the individual no doubt about it."

- Dr. Wayne Dyer

Everybody needs endorsement and acknowledgment from those we care about. Nonetheless, time and again we rely upon endorsement such a lot of that we neglect to focus on the main endorsement of all: our own.

Do you wind up concurring just to abstain from conflicting? Is it safe to say that you are continually searching out the endorsement of others before you pursue a choice? This endorsement fixation is harming to your journey for working on your life through certain reasoning. By taking care of your endorsement propensity, you become less dependent on your own contemplations and sentiments, and along these lines less on top of your objectives and what is genuinely best for you. However it's ideal to have the help of others, the main individual you can fulfil 100% of the time is you.

How might you kick the endorsement propensity and quit stressing over others' thought process of your activities? The following are a few activity plans you can continue to ensure your kin satisfying ability is utilized just where you maintain that it should be, and not as a brace for social acknowledgment.

Know Your Code

To try not to look for endorsement for the good of endorsement, you need to know your own convictions and norms. Monitoring what you trust in will assist you with voicing your viewpoints and pick the correct way for yourself, in any event, when others disagree. Fostering a solid moral code is a significant piece of the course of positive reasoning.

Recording your ethical code can assist with solidifying your goals and convictions and act as an aide for your dynamic cycle. Ponder the issues that are mean a lot to you. Do you accept family values precede all the other things? Is your vocation critical to you? What's the situation with legislative issues: could you rather be vocal in your convictions, or attempt to have an effect behind the scenes through casting a ballot? Your ethical code ought to oversee your activities in each circumstance, and you ought to never disregard your convictions just to acquire endorsement from another person.

Going to bat for what you have confidence in can be a necessary piece of assuming command over yourself and your life. At the point when you quit looking for endorsement or approval for your viewpoints in general and thoughts, you become a more grounded individual and individuals who genuinely care about you will regard and respect you for it, as opposed to dismissing. Be educated and foster your ethical code, then stick to it. You will be amazed at how much better you feel about yourself...and you won't require any other individual to second your perspective.

Move on from Secondary School

For the overwhelming majority of us, the requirement for acknowledgment started in secondary school. The craving to fit in areas of strength for is most teenagers, and by and large when you're in school there isn't anything more significant than companions. When we leave the designs bounds of school and enter the grown-up world, it tends to be hard to shake the inclination that you are just a commendable individual assuming you have a ton of companions, or the "right" companions.

As grown-ups, we really want to dispose of the unimportant social food chain of our school days. Life isn't a prevalence challenge. It may not astonish you to discover that the best grown-ups were misfits in school. A huge piece of the justification behind this is on the grounds that they didn't develop the acknowledgment of their companions, they were allowed to put resources into themselves, acquiring information and creating solid characters that didn't rely upon approval from the "in" swarm.

In the event that you want evidence, look at the accompanying rundown of fruitful individuals who battled through secondary school at the lower part of the natural pecking order:

• Henry Kissinger was designated "a little fatso" by a lot of people of his friends.

- Attractive entertainer and model Heather Graham was prodded continually for being calm and genuinely immature.
- Walt Disney was viewed as an indolent visionary who might never add up to anything by his educators and individual understudies.
- Eytan Sugarman-proprietor of the New York City club Calfskin which is visited by any semblance of Britney Lances, Cameron Diaz, and Leonardo DiCaprio-was a rotund and lonely kid whose life coaches let him know his life would go no place.

As a grown-up, you are substantially more equipped for understanding that peer acknowledgment doesn't make any difference beyond secondary school. You ought to endeavour to be consistent with yourself. Keep in mind, there is a spot for everybody it's a major planet.

Weed Your Companionship Nursery

A considerable lot of us will generally pass judgment on our value by the quantity of companions we have. In any case, this isn't generally an exact appraisal, and it tends to be tiring to stay aware of your get-togethers and Christmas card records especially when you have companions who you can't act naturally with.

Find opportunity to assess your fellowships. Are there individuals you invest energy with who appear to deplete you at whatever point you're around them? Do you continually feel like a fake while you're cooperating with them, and watch the clock until adequate time has elapsed so you can pardon yourself from the discussion? Companions are great to have, yet a few kinships simply do not merit developing.

The following time you wind up caught in an off-kilter circumstance and are hesitant to voice your actual contemplations, take a stab at expressing your real thoughts in any case. Almost certainly, one of two things will occur: either the individual you're chatting with will be keen on your viewpoint and you'll find the discussion moving into a certifiable area, or you will see an unexpected decrease in temperature and hear those reasons you as a rule make to get away from come from the other individual. In the event that the case is the previous, you have worked on your relationship and can loosen up around the individual; assuming it's the last option, you have quite recently freed yourself of a pointless channel on your energy and positive perspective.

Nothing bad can really be said about finishing companionships that simply aren't working out. Chances are, the other individual will be similarly however feeling better as you seem to be, and you can both fortify the connections you have with genuine companions. It will require an investment to separate the weeds from your kinship garden, yet everything will work out for the best for all interested parties. Liberating yourself from harming connections assists you with kicking the endorsement propensity as the need should arise "counterfeit it" to coexist with anybody.

Blood is thicker than Humiliation

It's one thing to cut off associations with companions, and very one more to do likewise with family. The majority of us are raised with the possibility that family is significant, and we will generally be more lenient of relatives as well as look for their endorsement for our activities more regularly. We are hesitant to act naturally around relatives.

In any case, attempt at finger pointing: Whose Shortcoming Is It?

"The explanation individuals pin things on the past age is that there's just a single other decision."

- Doug Larson

We are a general public driven by fault. We fault the public authority for running our lives, and our folks for destroying it. We fault the cheap food industry for making us fat, the tobacco business for giving us disease, and the equity framework for permitting lawbreakers to meander among us while blameless individuals sit in prison. We fault our youngsters for giving us silver hair, and our schools for outfitting our kids with the ways of behaving that make us old before our time. There is no off-base activity, incredible or little, for which we can't find another person to fault. The last individual we lay fault on is ourselves.

Again and again, however, we are the main individual we ought to highlight when issues emerge.

The public authority makes the guidelines however we are responsible for choosing the standard creators, and a large portion of us don't cast a ballot, while most of the people who do are deficiently informed. Our folks gigantically affect our lives-however they can raise us as well as they were prepared to by their own folks, and when we become grown-ups we are answerable for our own way of behaving. We decide to eat an excess of cheap food, smoke cigarettes, and attempt to escape discipline when we violate the law. Our youngsters' mirror our own conduct back at us like residing mirrors; and regardless of the amount of their time they spend in school, their way of behaving is resolved only by what we show them at home.

It depends on every single one of us to get a sense of ownership with our lives. Regardless of whether the wrongs in our lives were another person's shortcoming, we are the one that control our response to the circumstance. Whenever sad occasions happen in your life, you can decide to be furious and point fingers-or you can decide to take care of business. Be sure about who is at fault for the issues in your day to day existence, and do whatever it may take to address what is going on.

Making Your Omelette: How to Gain from Your Missteps

"Keep in mind: you just need to succeed the last time."

- Brian Tracy

No one's perfect. The uplifting news is: disappointment can really be great for you! The most effective way-and at times the best way to figure out how to make changes in your day to day existence and arrive at your objectives is by sorting out how to avoid things.

There is an interaction you can use to gain from your errors. The more you learn, the nearer you will be to arriving at your objectives throughout everyday life.

Give Yourself Consent

You realize you will commit errors, particularly in the event that you're attempting to accomplish something you've never finished. To be ready for the certainty of setbacks and misfortunes, let yourself know that when you commit an error, it's actually OK and you won't allow missteps to stop you.

This is important for the most common way of imparting a positive mentality. At the point when you know what's in store, it's harder for astonishments to impair you in your excursion to arrive at your objectives. Remember that it is good to commit errors, and doing not the apocalypse is as well. The main individuals who don't commit errors are individuals who don't attempt to do anything in any case. Try not to be the individual who laments never at any point attempting to achieve your objectives since you feared botches.

Commit Fascinating Errors

Yet again you will commit errors. At the point when this occurs, you will learn more by committing fascinating errors as opposed to dumb ones.

You might be thinking about what, precisely, is a fascinating misstep? The more perplexing and testing your definitive objective is, the more awesome your disappointments will be. The individual who encounters a marvellous disappointment is undeniably bound to acknowledge tremendous achievement. Here is a fast model:

Dumb Error: Slamming your toe on the rake you left lying in the yard.

Fascinating Slip-up: Turning $30 worth of powdered sugar and chocolate chips into unpalatable blocks while attempting to begin your sweets making organization since you misread the treats thermometer.

The main error will help you to take care of your instruments when you're finished utilizing them, yet this is the sort of thing you most likely ought to have definitely known. The subsequent slip-up, in any case, is undeniably more significant to you. It shows you how not to peruse a sweets thermometer, and you won't ever mess up the same way from this point onward. Presently you're one bit nearer to understanding your fantasy to begin a sweets making organization. What will your next botch be?

Fess Up

The capacity to concede that you've committed an error is pivotal to the educational experience. This doesn't be guaranteed to mean you need to declare your misstep to the world. Nonetheless, you really do need to be straightforward with yourself. Taking ownership of your missteps is significant, not just in that frame of mind to gain from them, yet in the whole course of utilizing positive reasoning. At the point when you concede your errors to yourself, be mindful so as not to cruelly pass judgment on your activities. Your considerations ought not to be in accordance with I messed this up, and I'm never going to get this right. Try not to allow your slip-ups to show you not to attempt. All things considered, think I committed an error, and presently I know to avoid that once more. The greatest example in committing errors can be tracked down in your getting a sense of ownership with them, and afterward effectively remedying what turned out badly.

Pinpoint Your Mistake

"For need of a nail, the horseshoe was lost..."

- Nursery rhyme (unknown)

Discussing what went wrong...do you know why you committed the error? You can't gain a single thing from your slip-ups on the off chance that you don't have any idea why it happened. Assuming things turn out badly, and it isn't obvious to you what occurred, backtrack along the way that carried you to the mistake and sort out where you wandered.

James R. Chiles, in his book Welcoming Fiasco: Stories from the Edge of Innovation, relates the shameful story of a drifting dorm in the North Ocean worked for seaward oil labourers. During one evening, the quarters turned over in the water and killed north of 100 individuals. The designers liable for building the residence hustled to track down a clarification, and at last found that one little break in the help structure, which had been covered up rather than appropriately fixed, was answerable for the chain of occasions prompting the catastrophe.

Finding the beginning of your own missteps will assist you with keeping away from expected calamity. Assume the liability to examine your missteps completely, so you can keep away from the compounding phenomenon one little mistake can have.

Discuss It

However you don't need to admit your missteps, it is in some cases supportive to talk over your issues with a thoughtful ear-especially in the event that that ear has a place with an individual who knows something about the objective you're attempting to reach.

Assuming you're experiencing difficulty overcoming something, requesting help checks out? Search out a specialist or somebody you realize who's had to deal with a similar encounter you're having, let them know what you feel you're fouling up, and pay attention to what they need to say. Frequently the most significant guidance we get comes from surprising sources, so go ahead and another person.

Can't see as a specialist? The basic demonstration of conversing with a companion or cherished one about your difficulties can be the impetus you want to continue onward in spite of your errors. You might have the option to work out precisely exact thing you want to change in your methodology as you talk about the thing you've been doing out loud; or you could basically wind up feeling loose, revived and prepared to handle the issue once more.

www.ingramcontent.com/pod-product-compliance
Lightning Source LLC
LaVergne TN
LVHW080556160826
845677LV00010B/1874

* 9 7 9 8 3 5 8 9 4 1 2 4 3 *